Reincarnation

Reincarnation

Exploring the Concept of
Reincarnation in Religion, Philosophy
and Traditional Cultures

Nevill Drury

BARNES
&NOBLE
BOOKS
NEW YORK

CONTENTS

Introduction

Have we lived on the Earth before? Do we continue to
reincarnate until we learn the spiritual lessons that life
teaches us in the "classroom" of everyday existence?
Is life itself an ongoing journey of the soul?

REINCARNATION IS UNDOUBTEDLY ONE of the most controversial spiritual beliefs, because it suggests that we have all lived many lives before, and probably have many more lives still ahead of us. It also implies that our individual personality – the person we identify with in our present life – is not really our true self. According to the doctrine of reincarnation, our individual personalities are just one aspect of a much broader and ongoing spiritual process of life, death, and rebirth.

Considered in this context, every human being is undertaking a spiritual journey – a journey of many lifetimes – and according to the Eastern wisdom teachings, this cycle of reincarnation cannot be broken until the individual reaches a state of spiritual liberation, or mystical transcendence. Until such a breakthrough is reached, each individual is destined to incarnate again and again. According to this particular approach, the cycle of rebirth cannot come to an end until the lessons of life have been learned in their entirety.

As we will see later in this book, several different types of evidence have emerged to support the concept of reincarnation. For example, from time to time, certain men and women have recounted details of past lives when they have been hypnotically regressed, and some of these individuals have spoken in the dialects or foreign languages of their former lives – languages completely unfamiliar in their present lifetime. Young children have also claimed to experience memories of previous incarnations, and in some instances have been taken by their parents to meet specific people to whom they may have been related in a former life. The possibility of reincarnation is one the major mysteries relating to our lives here on Earth. We can begin to explore this mystery in the first instance by asking this question: Why are we here?

Why are we here?

Some people believe that the world is essentially
meaningless, that our individual lives have come about by
chance, and that when we die – when our brain is no longer
functioning – we simply pass into nonexistence.

OTHERS BELIEVE THAT LIFE has a spiritual purpose, and that we can all use the
insights provided by our daily activities and our interactions with other human
beings and the world around us for our personal growth and spiritual
transformation. However, even if many of us incline more toward the second
perspective, the actual nature of people's spiritual beliefs varies considerably –
depending on which religious tradition has helped shape their individual
perspective and their basic spiritual assumptions.

Religions: East and West

One of the most important distinctions between the major Eastern and Western
religions is that Eastern traditions such as Hinduism and Buddhism emphasize
endless cycles of cosmic time without beginning or end, in which the Universe
and all living beings experience countless transformations. Western religions
such as Judaism, Christianity and Islam, on the other hand, conceive of the

Creation followed by a spiritual revelation and then a Final Judgment. Put simply, Eastern religions embrace infinite cycles of time, whereas Western religions deal with finite beginnings and endings. This different approach produces very different styles of religious belief. In the East, it is taken for granted that an individual has many lifetimes to achieve spiritual liberation; in the West there is only one opportunity – this lifetime – to achieve personal salvation and unity with God.

A follower of the Jewish, Christian or Muslim faiths is likely to believe that one's spiritual salvation depends very much on a personal decision to commit oneself to God, and that the consequences of this decision – made in the present lifetime – will last for all eternity. Most Jews, Christians and Muslims reject the idea of reincarnation completely, and maintain that we only have one life, given as a gift from God, in which to make the journey toward spiritual salvation. However, for followers of the major Eastern religious traditions, the concept of reincarnation is accepted as fundamentally true, and it is taken for granted that we all have numerous lifetimes in which to learn the spiritual lessons that everyday life presents. From this perspective, each new day brings fresh opportunities for insight and personal growth. With each new lifetime, we simply pick up where we left off last time around.

Karma and reincarnation

People who believe in reincarnation generally embrace the idea that we are all evolving as spiritual beings, and that our path through different physical incarnations leads us ever closer to a state of perfected awareness and spiritual self-realization. This means, essentially, that we are all masters of our own destiny – it is up to us to embrace the challenges and experiences of everyday life and learn from them.

In the East, belief in reincarnation is closely linked to the concept of karma – the idea that our individual positive or negative thoughts and actions will produce corresponding positive or negative consequences. The law of karma is based on the principle of cause and effect – the idea that for every action there is a reaction.

Most of us recognize this principle in the physical, everyday world, and most of us also acknowledge that our own actions and decisions will have consequences – that what we do now will have spin-off effects further down the line. However, the law of karma extends beyond the physical world, into the mental, emotional and spiritual aspects of life as well. It applies not only to our physical actions, but also to every conscious thought that we have. According to the karmic philosophy of life, positive thoughts and actions produce a positive outcome and create good karma. Negative thoughts and actions result in negative outcomes and create bad karma. Eastern spiritual teachings maintain that these positive or negative outcomes will present themselves at a later point in our present life, or in future incarnations.

Most people who believe in reincarnation accept that one lifetime simply isn't enough time to absorb and integrate all the lessons that human experience presents, and that it makes good sense to accept a succession of lives, or incarnations, as part of the journey toward spiritual self-realization.

According to this perspective, our individual human lives are very much part of a greater cycle of evolutionary spiritual development, and the seemingly endless cycle of individual births, deaths and rebirths ensures that all the lessons of life are finally learned and assimilated by us all.

So who actually believes in reincarnation, and what impact has this spiritual teaching had on modern Western culture? Is there any strong and convincing evidence that reincarnation is true, and are there different explanations for how the laws affecting reincarnation might actually work? We will consider all these topics and issues in turn, beginning with the role of reincarnation in world religion.

Reincarnation in world religion

Reincarnation is accepted as a fact of human existence by
many of the world's indigenous peoples, and also by many
leading world religions, including Hinduism, Buddhism, Taoism
and the Jain and Sikh traditions.

IN ADDITION, REINCARNATION BELIEFS are widely held by many who follow
New Age principles, and have also played a central role in the rise of theosophy
and the various forms of spiritualism, now more commonly known as
"channeling." Perspectives on reincarnation vary from place to place, and
traditions vary in their conception of the human soul and their point of view
about what actually reincarnates – the individual human consciousness, the
"subtle" or "spiritual" body, or God-consciousness itself.

Following is a summary of some of the main approaches to reincarnation.

HINDUISM

Sacred Hindu texts use the term *atman* to refer to the spiritual essence of a human being. In Hinduism, the atman is one's true self or universal self, because it connects each individual to the cosmos – to Brahman, the Supreme Reality. In Western culture, we tend to focus on the unique qualities of the individual personality. According to Hindu teaching, only the atman is real; the individual personality is illusory. Human beings tend to forget the nature of their special connection with Brahman, and they fall into *samsara* – the seemingly never-ending cycle of birth, life, death and rebirth. They are then destined to reincarnate until they realize their sacred origin. From a Hindu perspective, life is essentially a journey which takes us all back to the Supreme Being – the sacred Oneness of Brahman from which everything comes forth.

According to Hindu tradition, human souls can be differentiated according to the universal goals or "desires" that they pursue. For example, people pursuing a largely hedonistic or materialistic way of life may seek to immerse themselves substantially in pleasureable pursuits in order to avoid suffering, or they may become increasingly greedy in their desire for material wealth and personal power. However, according to the Hindu perspective, one can move from these more material goals toward the path of *dharma*, the path of moral and ethical conduct. Finally, one can learn to transcend physical and worldly considerations altogether and become one with the Spirit. In Hinduism, this state of awareness is known as *moksha*, or "liberation." Individuals who attain moksha are no longer bound by the chains of negative karma which result from ignorance and bad thoughts and deeds. In attaining the state of moksha, individuals become liberated from the cycle of life, death and rebirth, and therefore have no need to reincarnate any more.

There is also another Hindu perspective on reincarnation, according to which souls pass through mineral, vegetable and animal forms before becoming human. Later the human soul becomes angelic. Some Hindus also believe that it is possible for humans to regress from their present form and reincarnate as animals if their karma dictates it – a type of reincarnation in reverse. This particular form of reincarnation belief is sometimes known as transmigration, or metempsychosis. Most Buddhists, by way of comparison, reject this possibility altogether. Buddhists generally believe that once a soul has achieved human status the path of spiritual development continues ever upward toward spiritual release, and it is unlikely that a human being will revert to an animal form.

BUDDHISM

There are two main schools of Buddhism, known as Mahayana and Hinayana (or Theraveda). Mahayana Buddhism is found in northern India, Nepal, Japan, and Tibet; Hinayana Buddhism is more common in south-east Asia, in such countries as Thailand, Sri Lanka, Laos, and Burma.

Hinayana (or Theraveda) Buddhists do not embrace the Hindu teaching of the atman, and generally refer to "rebirth" rather than reincarnation. According to Theraveda Buddhists, the human soul isn't permanent – they reject the idea of an atman-connection to the God-consciousness. However, Theraveda Buddhists do believe that when a person dies, the general characteristics or qualities of the deceased individual will be transmitted to the life of a new person, so there is then a connection between these two incarnations.

Devotees of Mahayana Buddhism place special emphasis on the existence of Bodhisattvas – compassionate, spiritually enlightened individuals who have fully experienced the mystical state of Nirvana and who have no need to reincarnate, but who choose to return to earthly life to assist others less fortunate than themselves.

Tibetan Buddhists in particular are very specific about their belief in reincarnation, and regard their Dalai Lamas, or spiritual leaders, as Bodhisattvas. The present Dalai Lama, Tenzin Gyatso – the fourteenth leader in this spiritual succession – has frequently referred to his belief in past lives during his lectures and seminars. In his memoirs, *My Land and My People*, he mentions that it was his belief in karma and reincarnation which sustained him during the Chinese invasion of Tibet, and which helped him embrace compassion in the face of tragedy. "Belief in rebirth should engender a universal love," he writes, "... and the virtues our creed encourages are those which arise from this universal love – tolerance, forbearance, charity, kindness, compassion ... If there is no peace in one's mind, there can be no peace in one's approach to others, and thus no peaceful relations between individuals or between nations."

Since the fifteenth century it has been common in Tibet to search for reincarnations of important lamas, using oracles and divination and  identifying young children who have specific physical characteristics and memory patterns which seem to refer to previous incarnations. Gautama Buddha himself (c. 563–483 BC) – the founder of Buddhism – claimed to have experienced past lives, but he also taught his monks not to become too preoccupied with their previous incarnations, since this could become a distraction and lead them away from the true spiritual purpose of their present life.

JAINISM

Devotees of the ancient Indian Jain sect believe that their tradition is even older than Hinduism. Their main spiritual figurehead is Mahavira, who was a contemporary of Gautama Buddha.

Jains recognize the Hindu concept of samsara – the karmic cycle of rebirth – and they also believe in moksha, or spiritual enlightenment, as the means of escaping from this cycle. However, they differ from Hindus in focusing specifically on the karmic consequences of particular actions, not the moral intent of the actions. For example, according to the Jain perspective, killing someone unintentionally and murdering someone in cold blood would produce an identical karmic result. Jains also believe that souls have to reside in a human body, so after death they immediately attach themselves to a newly conceived child, in order to be reborn nine months later.

THE SIKHS

The Sikh religion was founded by Guru Nanak (1469–1593), and combines elements of Hinduism and Islam. Guru Nanak held that he himself had been born many times – as a tree, a bird and an animal – and that in past lives he had performed both evil and meritorious deeds.

Sikhs follow Hindu beliefs about karma and reincarnation, but believe that spiritual release from the cycle of rebirth comes both from one's own individual efforts and by the grace of God. According to Guru Nanak, the individual who seeks spiritual enlightenment through personal effort will be continually reborn – it is only through God's grace that a human being can achieve final spiritual liberation.

TAOISM

The great Chinese sage Confucius (c. 551–479 BC) always avoided meta-physical speculation and would not be drawn into a discussion about immortality or spiritual rebirth. However, the philosopher and teacher Lao-Tzu – a contemporary of Confucius – believed in the eternity of the Tao (the unity underlying the apparently conflicting phenomena of the universe); he is recognized as the founder of Taoism. His disciple, Chuang Tzu, seems to have embraced the idea of a spiritual essence surviving death, and wrote in one of his texts:

> *Death and life are not far apart … When I look for their origin,*
> *it goes back into infinity; when I look for their end, it proceeds without*
> *termination … Life is the follower of death, and death is*
> *the predecessor of life …*

When Buddhism began to spread into China from the first century AD onward, it was the Taoist followers of Lao-Tzu and Chuang Tzu who responded most positively to the Buddhist idea of spiritual rebirth. Today, many Chinese Taoists believe in the possibility of reincarnation.

NATIVE SPIRITUALITY

Different types of reincarnation belief are widely embraced by indigenous groups in different parts of the world. Many tribal peoples in Africa, for example, believe that human beings are reincarnated as human beings or animals, and some Zulus believe that after death the soul is part-human and part-beast.

The Sea Dyaks of Indonesia believe that the human soul dies many times, and eventually becomes an insect or a jungle plant, while the Aranda (also known as the Arunta, Arrente, or Arrernte) Aborigines of central Australia maintain that the souls of their ancestors enter their sacred churingas (a sacred object used during ceremonial initiations) and are later reborn as new individuals within their Dreamtime territories.

The Canadian Gitksan Indians of British Columbia look for specific birthmarks to determine which of their ancestors have been reincarnated. These birthmarks may relate to wounds or deformities associated with particular ancestors. Sometimes, too, Gitksan ancestors announce in dreams that they will soon be reborn.

Reincarnation beliefs were also common among the Iroquois, Dakota, Huron, Kiowa and Hopi Indians in the United States.

Reincarnation in Western culture

Belief in past lives is now common among people
who embrace New Age perspectives, and the idea of
reincarnation is not new to the West.

THE ANCIENT EGYPTIANS WERE attracted to the concept of spiritual rebirth; so too were the Greeks and Romans of Classical times. It goes without saying that all these great civilizations have had a profound influence on the development of our Western spiritual and philosophical heritage.

Reincarnation in ancient Egypt

In ancient Egypt the so-called "ka-name" or "soul-name" of King Amonemhat I was "He who repeats births," while the ka-name of Setekhy I was "Repeater of births." There are also references in the Egyptian Book of the Dead to spells that guaranteed that the soul of a person who had just died would be reborn in certain specific forms. The goal of every Egyptian was to avoid the uncertainties and terrors of the underworld and to journey after death to the realm of the Sun God. This in turn gave rise to spiritual beliefs which supported both resurrection and reincarnation – both these ideas are a variation on the concept of spiritual rebirth, and relate to the survival and future life of the soul after death.

In one version of this belief, the deceased soul went to dwell in the Field of Aaru, sustained by Osiris, God of Fertility and Lord of the Underworld. In a variation on this theme, the human soul was believed to journey for all eternity in the presence of the Sun God – a journey which would repeat itself through the twelve hours of daylight and the twelve hours of the night-time, the latter regarded as the twelve gates of the Underworld. With the dawn of each new day, the human soul traveling with the Sun God would emerge triumphantly from the terrors of darkness – here the concept of spiritual survival was associated with the theme of "coming forth by day." This process of daily rebirth would continue for eternity.

Ancient Greece and Rome

According to the historian Herodotus (c. 485–425 BC), the ancient Greeks learned about reincarnation from the Egyptians. Devotees of the Orphic Mysteries were taught that the body is a prison which traps the immortal soul during one's individual lifetime.

However, according to the Orphics, the soul itself would always yearn to be free, and after death would feel completely liberated until commencing its next incarnation – when it re-entered the "prison" of physical existence.

Several famous Greek philosophers openly embraced the idea of reincarnation. The well-known mathematician Pythagoras (sixth century BC) used to say that in a past life he had been Aethalides, son of the god Mercury, and was then reborn as Euphorbus, who was fatally wounded during the siege of Troy. Later he became Pyrrus, a fisherman, before being reincarnated as Pythagoras.

Plato (427–347 BC), perhaps the most famous Greek philosopher of all, believed in the immortality of the soul, and also maintained that life itself consisted of a fixed number of souls. These souls would take different forms, according to the cycles and patterns of Nature – some souls would be reborn as animals, others as humans. In his book *The Republic*, Plato mentions a soldier named Er who was wounded and left to die on the battlefield. Er had what we would nowadays call a "near-death experience," and returned to life twelve days later, but during the twelve days he witnessed a number of human souls choosing to reincarnate in a human form while others chose to be reborn as animals.

We are also told, in relation to these discarnate souls (souls having no physical body), that the experience of their former life "guided the choice" of their next incarnation. However, when these souls had made their decision about their next life, they would journey to the plain of Forgetfulness and drink from the river of Indifference, thereby dissolving all memories of their former incarnations, before being carried, "like shooting stars," toward their next birth.

Other notable Greek thinkers who believed in reincarnation include the poet Pindar (c. 522–440 BC), the philosopher Heraclitus of Ephesus (writing c. 500 BC), and the statesman Empedocles (c. 492–432 BC), who once wrote:

"I was once already boy and girl, thicket and bird, and mute fish in the waves. All things doth Nature change, enwrapping souls in unfamiliar tunics of the flesh."

The teachings of Plato and Pythagoras had a major impact on the Roman world, and several leading Roman thinkers espoused reincarnation ideas. The famous Roman orator Cicero (106–43 BC) proclaimed that "the ancients ... seem to have known the truth, when they affirmed that we were born into the body to pay the penalty for sins committed in a former life." Similarly, the Roman poet Ovid (43 BC–17 AD) wrote in *Metamorphoses* that "the immortal soul flies out into empty space, to seek her fortune in some other place." The Roman emperor Julian (331–363 AD), meanwhile, regarded himself as a reincarnation of Alexander the Great (356–323 BC).

Other famous figures

Many other famous figures in Western history have been attracted to the idea of reincarnation. Here is a selection of views and opinions from influential thinkers who have embraced the concept of spiritual rebirth ...

Louisa May Alcott (1832–88)
American novelist

I think immortality is the passing of the soul through many lives or experiences, and such as are truly lived, used, and learned, help on to the next, each growing richer, happier and higher, carrying with it only the real memories of what has gone before ...

Frederick the Great (1712–86)
King of Prussia

... I feel that soon I shall have done with my earthly life. Now, since I am convinced that nothing existing in Nature can be annihilated, so I know for a certainty that the more noble part of me will not cease to live. Though I may not be a king in my future life, so much the better: I shall nevertheless live an active life ...

GUSTAVE FLAUBERT (1821–80)
FRENCH NOVELIST

I don't experience … this feeling of a life which is beginning, the stupefaction of a newly commenced existence. It seems to me, on the contrary, that I have always lived! And I possess memories which go back to the Pharaohs. I see myself very clearly at different ages of history, practicing different professions and in many sorts of fortune. My present personality is the result of my lost personalities …

HENRY FORD (1863–1947)
AMERICAN INDUSTRIALIST

When I discovered Reincarnation it was as if I had found a universal plan. I realized that there was a chance to work out my ideas. Time was no longer limited. I was no longer a slave to the hands of a clock… I would like to communicate to others the calmness that the long view of life gives us.

THOMAS CARLYLE (1795–1881)
SCOTTISH HISTORIAN AND ESSAYIST

… though all dies, and even gods die, yet all death is but a phoenix fire-death, and new-birth into the Greater and the Better!

Victor Hugo (1802–85)
French Novelist

*Each time we die we gain more of life. Souls pass from
one sphere to another without loss of personality, become more
and more bright … The whole creation is a perpetual ascension,
from brute to man, from man to God. To divest ourselves more and
more of matter, to be clothed more and more with spirit …*

Leibniz (1646–1716)
German Philosopher

*… all bodies are in a perpetual flux like rivers,
and parts are passing in and out of them continually.*

Richard Wagner (1813–83)
German Composer

*In contrast to reincarnation and karma,
all other views appear petty and narrow.*

William Wordsworth (1770–1850)
English poet

Our birth is but a sleep and a forgetting;
The Soul that rises with us, our life's Star,
Hath had elsewhere its setting,
And cometh from afar.

Gustav Mahler (1860–1911)
German composer

We all return; it is this certainty that gives meaning to life,
and it does not make the slightest difference whether or
not in a later incarnation we remember the former life.
What counts is not the individual and his comfort, but the
great aspiration to the perfect and the pure which goes
on in each incarnation.

Napoleon Bonaparte (1769–1821)
Emperor of France

I am Charlemagne. Do you know who I am?
I am Charlemagne … Tell the Pope that I am keeping my eyes open;
tell him that I am Charlemagne, the Sword of the Church,
his Emperor, and as such I expect to be treated.

Why believe in reincarnation?

Even though numerous devotees of Eastern religious
traditions believe in reincarnation, and it was also embraced by
Classical philosophers in the past, this doesn't in itself mean
that reincarnation occurs.

THERE IS NO AUTOMATIC NEED for us to take it on trust, or accept it as a matter
of faith. As Gautama Buddha advised his monks, it is always best to examine any
religious or philosophical teaching individually, preferably on the basis of

personal experience, before accepting it as valid or rejecting it. If we take this approach, we should examine the evidence for claimed reincarnation cases ourselves, and only then decide whether or not we can accept reincarnation as true.

It is also clear that different groups of people and different religious traditions reject the idea of reincarnation for quite different reasons. For followers of Judaism, Christianity and Islam, belief in reincarnation belongs outside the realm of doctrinal orthodoxy and is therefore unacceptable.

Meanwhile, for most contemporary scientists – in particular, those scientists who only accept physical reality – there is no reason to believe in reincarnation or any other form of spiritual teaching, because the human soul, or spirit, simply doesn't exist. Let's explore these perspectives in a little more detail.

Judaism, Christianity and Islam

Judaism, Christianity and Islam share this much in common: they all focus on the concept of God's Creation, including the unique creation of each human soul, and they all emphasize a process of spiritual salvation or redemption which leads to a state of union with God. They also maintain that, after our lives on Earth, those of us who have received spiritual salvation will have the opportunity to return to live in Heaven with the Creator to whom we owe our very existence.

In the Jewish spiritual tradition, God the Creator is known as JHVH – his sacred name is generally transcribed as Jehovah or Yahweh. Orthodox Jews, however, avoid uttering this sacred name aloud, out of reverence for the Holy One, and instead refer to God as "Adonai" (Lord). Many Jews continue to await the arrival of a Messiah who will show suffering humanity the path back to God.

For Christians, Jesus Christ is one with God the Father and the Holy Spirit, and spiritual salvation involves accepting Christ as their personal savior. Christians believe that when they die they will go to Heaven and be at one with Christ for all eternity.

Muslims acknowledge both Judaism and Christianity as precursors of their own religious tradition, but believe that Muhammad was the final prophet sent by the one true God – Allah – and that the Koran therefore contains the final and most complete spiritual revelation available to humanity. Muslims who diligently pursue the five essential duties – the confession of faith, prayer, almsgiving, fasting and spiritual pilgrimage – expect to spend eternity in Paradise.

In all three traditions – Judaism, Christianity and Islam – the believer is expected to make a choice for spiritual salvation in the present lifetime, for this is the only life we have, and each individual human life, or soul, comes directly from God. The idea of spiritual salvation occurring in a future lifetime simply does not arise. Indeed, one could hardly expect reincarnation to be acceptable

within any of these mainstream religious traditions — such a teaching would weaken the sense of urgency associated with the need for exclusive spiritual salvation. Why emphasize the need for salvation in this lifetime if future lifetimes lie ahead?

Reincarnation and Christian heresy

Interestingly, the concept of reincarnation was accepted by some early Church Fathers, such as Justin Martyr (100–165 AD) and Origen (185–254 AD), both of whom had been influenced by the Greek philosopher Plato. Origen, in particular, openly advocated the pre-existence of the soul — the idea that the soul exists before birth. However, following the first two Ecumenical meetings of Church bishops — at Nicaea in 325 AD and Constantinople in 381 AD — Catholic orthodoxy was established and pre-Christian pagan perspectives condemned. Origen's concept of the pre-existence of the soul continued to influence a number of theologians and philosophers, but was finally rejected as a heresy at the Second Council of Constantinople, in 553 AD. And any possibility that reincarnation could be a part of the Christian doctrine was finally eliminated at the Council of Lyons in 1274 AD, when it was officially stated that after death the Christian soul would go immediately to Heaven, Purgatory or Hell. Belief in past or future lives was totally rejected, as being contrary to Christian teachings.

Reincarnation and materialism

The other main group of people who deny the possibility of reincarnation are so-called materialists – individuals who maintain that our material, or physical, world is the only "reality" that exists. Most materialists are atheists – people who deny the existence of a personal God. However, some materialists describe themselves as agnostics, staying open to the possibility that the existence of God could perhaps one day be logically or scientifically proven.

The so-called materialist concept of reality, a world view widely embraced by modern scientists, has its origins in the ideas of Sir Isaac Newton and René Descartes. According to this model of reality, the basic elements of the universe are solid and ultimately indestructible. The fundamental building blocks of matter – atoms – are subject to gravity and the laws of cause and effect. For materialists, the physical world is the only realm in which we can hope to find any sense of meaning, or any logical explanation, for our existence, if indeed there is any meaning to life at all. Materialist scientists who seek to explain the origins of human awareness look to the brain for a complete explanation of the full range of human functioning. According to this perspective, all human responses, including intuition, empathy, love, creativity and inspiration, are simply the result of human brain chemistry, and there is no need to involve such concepts as the human soul or 'spirit.'

By definition, materialists cannot accept the concept of life after death. From a materialist perspective, when the brain dies conscious awareness also dies; there is nothing relating to the individual identity that survives and lives on after death. From this perspective, our only chance for immortality rests with the legacy of our DNA, which we pass on to our offspring! And the human soul going to Heaven or Hell, or, alternatively, reincarnating at some future time, is impossible. A materialist is obliged to reject all religious or spiritual concepts of an afterlife.

So who is correct? Are science and reincarnation completely at odds with each other, or can they be reconciled? Is there any scientific or experiential evidence for past lives? These are the issues we will now address in more detail.

Reincarnation memories in young children

Some of the best evidence relating to reincarnation can be
found in the memories of young children.
If a child claims to its parents that it has lived an earlier life in a
specific, distant location and goes on to
name individual relatives and characteristics of the family
home, without ever having visited the locality in question, this
is very compelling evidence.

YOUNG CHILDREN – CHILDREN UNDER the age of five or six years, for example –
are less worldly than teenagers and adults, have scant access to information from
other regions and localities, and would have little motive or personal capacity to
fabricate evidence. So reincarnation evidence from young children is always of
considerable interest, especially when there is a possibility of verifying the claims
these children make.

Shanti Devi

One of the most famous cases of this type involved a girl called Shanti Devi, who was born in Delhi in October 1926. From the age of three, Shanti began to recall and state details of a former life in the town of Muttra, around 80 miles away. She said her name had been Lugdi, that she had been born in 1902, and had been married to a cloth merchant named Kedar Nath Chaubey. She also said that she had given birth to a son and had died ten days later.

Shanti continued to make these statements, and, some time later, when she was nine, her grand-uncle decided to try to find out whether such a person as Kedar Nath Chaubey actually existed in Muttra. This man was eventually located, and was able to confirm that Shanti's claims seemed to be correct. However, to find out for himself, Chaubey sent his cousin, Sri Lal, to the girl's house, and later came himself, unannounced. Shanti immediately identified both of them.

In 1936, after it had been established that Shanti Devi had never left Delhi in her present life, she was taken by a committee of investigators to Muttra, so that they could observe her responses firsthand. At Muttra railway station Shanti recognized a relative of Kedar Nath Chaubey in a large crowd.

Later she drove in a carriage through the district where she said she had lived in her former life, guiding the driver by giving him instructions about where to go. As she approached the Chaubey family house she was able to identify it, even though it had since been painted a different color. Shanti subsequently correctly answered several questions relating to the arrangement of the rooms and closets, and also correctly identified a location where some money had been buried. She also used expressions of speech familiar only in Muttra, despite the fact that she had never had any exposure to this particular dialect.

Shanti Devi made no incorrect statements relating to her claimed former incarnation as the wife of Kedar Nath Chaubey. The case remains one of the most interesting in the annals of reincarnation research.

Prabhu Khairti

In 1923 a four-year-old Indian boy named Prabhu Khairti similarly began to claim that he had lived a previous life in another town some distance away. His statements were documented and then investigated by officials from the State government in Bharatpur.

Prabhu said that his name had previously been Harbux Braham, and he had lived in the village of Hatyori. He had three brothers, one of whom had died, and two sons, Ghure and Sham Lal. Prabhu said he also had two daughters, Kokila and Bholi, and was able to name his daughters' husbands.

Prabhu described details of his house in Hatyori, and the home adjoining it, which belonged to a person named Swarupa Jat. He also provided details of a nearby tank, gave a description of the raised pathway which led up to his house, and referred to a domed cenotaph located nearby. He also mentioned two pipal trees and various drinking wells located near his home, and referred to an inscription on a fortress in Hatyori "with a serpent on it."

Prabhu said his father was called Munde, his maternal uncle Bargawan, and his wife Ganjo. He also mentioned that his father-in-law, Moola Jat, had once fallen into a well but he (Harbux Braham) had managed to help bring him out alive. Prabhu went on to describe how he had died in a bungalow outside his village, predeceasing his father.

When the Bharatpur authorities assessed Prabhu's statements and checked their accuracy, they found that of 36 specific items, two could not be checked either way, 29 were correct and five did not match. However, the officials were impressed by the accuracy of some of the unusual details in Prabhu's account – for instance, inquiries revealed that the wife's real name was Gaura, but because she was slightly bald she had been nicknamed Ganjo, which means "bald-headed."

The Pollock twins

Another well-known reincarnation case is that of the Pollock twins in England. John and Florence Pollock lived with their two daughters – Joanna, aged eleven, and Jacqueline aged six – in the town of Hexham, Northumberland. The family was Catholic and the girls attended the local church each Sunday. On 5 May 1957 the two girls set out with a school friend, Anthony Layden, to walk to their local church. On the way all three were struck by a car, tossed into the air, and killed immediately.

Although he had converted to Catholicism when he was nineteen, John Pollock had always had an interest in reincarnation and so now, following the tragic loss of his daughters, he prayed to God to seek evidence for the truth of reincarnation.

A few months later, when Florence told her husband she was pregnant, John confidently predicted that she would have twins and that these twins would be the reincarnations of Joanna and Jacqueline.

Like John, Florence was also a convert to Catholicism, but unlike her husband she found the concept of reincarnation completely abhorrent. Neither his side of the family nor hers had a history of twins.

Nevertheless, Florence did give birth to twin daughters, on 4 October 1958, and the Pollocks named them Gillian and Jennifer. John was convinced that his first daughters had returned, and noticed that Jennifer had a scar-like mark on her forehead which resembled a scar that Jacqueline had received when she fell off her bicycle. Jennifer also had a birthmark on her left hip which was virtually identical to Jacqueline's birthmark.

When the twins were about four months old the Pollocks moved from Hexham to Whitley Bay – around 30 miles away – and did not return to

Hexham until three years later. However, the girls' parents were amazed when the twins seemed to recognize their former school and also the house where they had lived before. A year later, John Pollock took out some dolls which had been put away after the deaths of Joanna and Jacqueline. Gillian and Jennifer immediately recognized them, referring to them by the names which Joanna and Jacqueline had given them.

The reincarnation research of Dr. Ian Stevenson

For many years, cases such as those of Shanti Devi, Prabhu Khairti and the Pollock twins have been a consuming interest of Dr. Ian Stevenson, Alumni Professor of Psychiatry at the University of Virginia School of Medicine. Over a period spanning several decades, Professor Stevenson and his staff have traveled to numerous countries seeking reincarnation evidence – they have visited India, Sri Lanka, Brazil, Lebanon, Turkey and Thailand, and Tlingit Indian communities in southeastern Alaska, where a number of reincarnation cases have been reported. Professor Stevenson has now documented more than 2000 cases of claimed reincarnational memories in young children, and has published his findings in a number of scholarly books and journals.

An analysis of these cases suggests that reincarnational memories in the children of different cultures are remarkably similar – even in isolated communities that have little contact with other cultural groups.

Professor Stevenson does not take all these cases on face value, and has stated that in some instances other factors – telepathy, "racial memory," and sometimes even fraud – may also be involved. However, it is not only the reincarnation accounts themselves which interest him. He is also interested in birthmarks which may appear to correspond to bullet or stab wounds from previous lives, and has explored the issue of whether a violent death is likely to lead to a more hasty reincarnation than would otherwise be the case. The Tlingit Indians, for example, believe it is better to be killed than to die a natural death, because this will ensure a better and faster rebirth. Interestingly, by way of comparison, members of the Druse sect in Lebanon believe that a dead person's spirit will be reincarnated immediately after death, regardless of how a person dies, and that there is no time delay between successive lives.

The Dalai Lama and reincarnation

One of the most fascinating examples of tracing
reincarnation patterns through children occurs in Tibet.
The Dalai Lama is the spiritual and political leader of the
Tibetan people, and each Dalai Lama is regarded as a
reincarnation, or tulku, of the preceding Dalai Lama.

AFTER THE DEATH OF a Dalai Lama it is very important that a young child be located who shows clear signs of being the reincarnation of the former spiritual leader. In Tibet a Regent is appointed by the National Assembly to govern the country until the identified child attains maturity and can be formally invested as the nation's ruler.

Finding the tulku

In the Tibetan Mahayana Buddhist tradition a *tulku* is a person who is recognized as the reincarnation of a specific person who has died. According to French travel writer and Buddhist Alexandra David-Neel, some Tibetans extend the concept of the tulku to include reincarnations not only of human beings but also of gods, demons and fairies. For all Tibetans, however, the tulku of the Dalai Lama is an extremely special reincarnation. Locating the tulku who will become recognized as the next Dalai Lama is crucially important in preserving the sense of the spiritual lineage which sustains Tibet itself.

There have been fourteen Dalai Lamas in succession since the first, Gendun Drub, who lived in the fifteenth century. The title "Dalai Lama" means "a teacher whose wisdom is as great as the ocean." The present Dalai Lama, Tenzin Gyatso, was born in 1935. Following the Chinese invasion of Tibet, he has lived in self-imposed exile in Dharamsala in northern India, but continues to exercise a spiritual authority that is binding on the Tibetan people.

Bodhisattvas

All Dalai Lamas are regarded as being bodhisattvas – enlightened beings who have chosen to incarnate in order to assist the spiritual progress of those less fortunate than themselves. Each Dalai Lama is also considered to be an incarnation of Avalokiteshvara, the Compassionate One – one of the most important bodhisattvas in Tibetan Buddhism. So far all Dalai Lamas have been male, and all have been born in Tibet except for one who was a native of Mongolia. However, in theory there is no reason why a Dalai Lama couldn't be female, or be born in a country some distance away from Tibet.

Tenzin Gyatso is believed to be a reincarnation of Thupten Gyatso, who died in 1933, two years before the present Dalai Lama was born. After Thupten Gyatso died, many monks went forth looking for evidence of a new incarnation of "the holy one" – a child able to recognize personal objects that belonged to his predecessor and who could pick them out unerringly from a range of similar objects. At the age of three, Tenzin Gyatso was identified as the reincarnation of

Thupten Gyatso because he was able to demonstrate this specific connection with the former spiritual leader. When the young child caught sight of these particular personal objects – which included rosaries, drums and a walking stick – he called out, "They're mine, they're mine!" He was soon accepted as the tulku the monks had been looking for and in due course was taken away from his family home and brought to a monastery to begin his spiritual education for future leadership. This took place in 1938, and he was officially invested with spiritual authority as leader of the Tibetan people in 1950.

The present Dalai Lama draws a distinction between rebirth and reincarnation. According to the Tibetan Buddhist concept of everyday life, all human beings are swept along in the seemingly endless cycle of life, death and rebirth known as samsara. This cycle is determined by the Law of Karma – a person cannot be liberated from this cycle of karmically determined rebirths until he or she has become enlightened. So rebirth is regarded simply as a function of human existence.

However, when an enlightened being, a bodhisattva, chooses to enter into a new incarnation for the purpose of helping suffering humanity, this is an act which is specifically intended – a deliberate reincarnation. The Dalai Lama has explained, through the numerous interviews he has given around the world, that this type of reincarnation is far less common than general rebirth. As the Dalai Lama told French film writer Jean-Claude Carrière during one such interview, "The cycle of rebirths, samsara, is the very condition of all life. No existence escapes it, unless it gets to *nirvana*. This condition is painful, because it obliges us to live and live again, on levels that can be worse than those we have known. If rebirth is an obligation, reincarnation is a choice. It is the power, granted to certain worthy individuals, to control their future birth."

The coarse and subtle mind

According to the Dalai Lama, most ordinary human beings – especially those attracted to a consumerist or materialistic lifestyle – live their lives on a "coarse" or unsubtle level of mental awareness. People who practice meditation or yoga, on the other hand, begin to open themselves to what he refers to as "the subtle mind" or "subtle consciousness." The Dalai Lama says it is the subtle mind that reincarnates, not the soul – because soul, or atman – is by its very nature constant and timeless, and has no need to reincarnate. At the subtle level of mystical awareness, however, the meditator becomes aware of the cyclic journey of human consciousness, a journey which has no beginning and no end.

If this is so, one may reasonably ask, is it possible to specifically recall our past lives as the Buddha himself is supposed to have done? According to the Dalai Lama it is indeed possible to recall "... not [only] one life, but hundreds, thousands of lives. The mind can't be born from anything except mind. Consequently the subtle mind can't have a beginning. When the subtle consciousness appears in all its clarity, the questions aren't raised in the same way, the very idea of a beginning disappears."

Some classic cases of reincarnation

We have already referred to the ongoing reincarnation research
of Dr. Ian Stevenson, which has tended to focus mainly on
evidence based on reincarnation memories in young children.
More recently, Dr. Stevenson has also begun to explore what
he calls the relationship between biology and reincarnation.

BIRTHMARK REINCARNATION EVIDENCE IS especially prevalent among the Inuits
(or Eskimos) and the Tlingit Indians of Alaska. Both the Tlingits and the Inuits
are familiar with violent death and with wounds caused by savage attacks from
wild animals. They also report frequent injuries inflicted by spears, guns, knives
or axes as the result of fights. Dr. Stevenson has explored several hundred cases
where the birthmarks that appear on a person's body are claimed to be linked to
surgical procedures or stab and bullet wounds which occurred in previous lives.

The scars of Victor Vincent

A case in point is that of Victor Vincent. Victor was a full-blooded Tlingit Indian who lived on an island in southern Alaska. In 1946, toward the end of his life, he became very close to his niece, Mrs. Corliss Chotkin – the daughter of his sister – and told her that after he died he would be reborn as her next son. Vincent also maintained that she would know it was him because her newborn son would bear two birthmarks related to scars that Vincent had on his body. Vincent had a very distinctive scar on his back, and another on the right side of his nose near its base. He told Mrs. Chotkin that he would imprint these scars onto the body of his next incarnation to prove that he had indeed been reborn.

In December 1947, fifteen months after her uncle Victor died, Mrs. Chotkin gave birth to a son, whom she named Corliss Junior – the baby was born with birthmarks in exactly the same locations as Victor Vincent's scars. The scar near the boy's nose became less noticeable as he grew older but the mark on his back became even more distinctive, and had all the characteristics of a surgical incision that had healed over: it was raised and pigmented and also itched like a wound on the mend.

When the boy was just over a year old he began to utter his first words, and around the age of thirteen months he said to his mother, "Don't you know me? I'm Kahkody." This was Victor Vincent's tribal name, and Mrs. Chotkin was amazed that her son seemed to speak with the same accent as her deceased uncle. Later, when he was two and being wheeled along the street in Sitka, where the family lived, Corliss Junior spontaneously recognized one of Victor Vincent's stepdaughters and called her correctly by her name, Susie. Later that year he recognized Victor Vincent's son William, who was visiting Sitka unannounced, and said to his mother, "There is William, my son."

At the age of three Corliss Junior identified Victor Vincent's widow, Rose, in a large crowd – spotting her even before Mrs. Chotkin had noticed her – and on another occasion he recognized a close family friend of Victor's who happened to be in Sitka at the time. Later he identified other friends of Victor's, referring to them correctly by their tribal names.

By the age of nine, however, Corliss was able to recall fewer and fewer memories of his former life, and by the age of fifteen he could recall nothing at all from his previous incarnation. Indeed, in most cases such as this, the memories of past lives seem to disappear with the passage of the time. It is with good reason that Dr. Stevenson seeks to document the evidence of reincarnational memories in young children – before the evidence is lost.

The "life readings" of Edgar Cayce

Edgar Cayce is one the most famous psychics and reincarnationists of all time, and yet belief in reincarnation was not part of his religious upbringing.

Edgar Cayce was born on March 18, 1877 in Kentucky. He came from a fundamentalist Protestant Christian background. As a young man, Cayce discovered that he could give accurate healing diagnoses for other people by going into a hypnotic trance. Here he would be assisted by inner guidance toward the diagnosis of diseases, often using medical terms which were completely unknown to him. On one occasion he gave a diagnosis in fluent Italian, even though he was not familiar with this language in his everyday waking consciousness. This remarkable psychic gift led him in turn to giving "life readings" – readings which seemed to reveal the existence of past lives and their karmic influence on present-day health problems.

It came as something of a shock to Edgar Cayce when his subconscious mind began to alert him to the possibility of past lives and reincarnation. He was familiar with the concept of psychic potentials – clairvoyance, telepathy, precognition and the power of prophecy – but reincarnation seemed too fantastic to be credible. It was also contrary to his Christian beliefs.

In 1923 Cayce traveled to Dayton, Ohio, to meet a man named Arthur Lammers. This meeting would change his approach to psychic diagnosis forever. Lammers was interested in the occult, and it seemed to him that if Cayce could correctly diagnose ailments by going into trance, he might also be able to uncover the metaphysical secrets of life, death and spiritual development. Lammers asked Cayce if he had ever sought to discover our true purpose on Earth, the nature of the soul, and what we were doing before each of us was born.

Cayce didn't have an immediate answer for Lammers and was somewhat taken aback because until this point he had used the Bible as his sole source of spiritual authority. Cayce nevertheless agreed to explore these issues further, and gave Lammers a trance reading. The reading revealed that Lammers had been a monk in a past life. Cayce also began to use Sanskrit terms such as "karma" and "akasa," which he had never used before. From this time onwards, Cayce's trance readings would frequently refer to past lives, and would often use mystical terminology to explain the secrets of the spiritual world.

As a result of his meeting with Lammers, Cayce also agreed to use the following formula as the basis of his life readings while he was in a state of trance: "You will have before you [name] born [date] in/at [place of birth]. You will give the relation of this entity and the universe and the universal forces, giving the conditions which are as personalities, latent and exhibited, in the present life; also the former appearances on the earth plane, giving time, place and the name; and that in each life which built or retarded the entity's development."

The idea of these life readings was to reveal both the positive and negative influences that past lives had brought to bear on one's present existence. The readings would also demonstrate how certain attitudes and personality characteristics were specifically connected to previous incarnations.

Cayce soon discovered that many of his present friends had been relatives or associates in a previous life. He also learned, psychically, that he had been an Egyptian high priest named Rata in a former incarnation and that his present wife, Gertrude, had been his wife in ancient Egypt as well. In other incarnations, Edgar Cayce had been a Persian physician, an Arab tribal leader named Uhjltd, and the biblical figure Lucius – a relative of Luke and a friend of Paul. He had also incarnated in 1742 as John Bainbridge, a gambler, libertarian and soldier in the British army who had been stationed in America prior to the War of Independence. His present lifetime, as Edgar Cayce, had been given to him as an opportunity to make up for the sensual excesses and materialism of his previous life as John Bainbridge.

One could easily dismiss Edgar Cayce's past-life experiences simply as delusional fantasies if his legacy amounted to just a small number of isolated psychic impressions. However, it is the enormous number of life readings made for other people which has secured Edgar Cayce's enduring reputation as a psychic and healer. Here are two typical examples from the Cayce archives.

David Greenwood was fourteen years old when Edgar Cayce gave him his life reading, on August 29, 1927. Cayce told Greenwood about five previous incarnations. The first of these could be traced to a time prior to 10,000 BC, when he had been Amiaie-Oulieb, heir to the throne in Atlantis. Then, around 10,000 BC, Greenwood had been an Egyptian named Isois, and he had served as a lay preacher and as an intermediary between his own people and the conquering ruler-class. Later he was Abiel, a court physician in Persia; and in his fourth incarnation he was Colval, a tradesman who abused his position of power in the Greek city of Salonika. Finally he had served both Louis XIII and Louis XIV of France as a loyal Master of Robes. Cayce warned Greenwood about his digestive problems and quick temper, and told him to pursue a trade related to clothing or materials. Despite having no personal interest in this field, David Greenwood became a salesman in a clothing company in 1940, and proved to be very successful in this role. He also suffered from food allergies, and was obliged to take Edgar Cayce's advice by adhering to a strict diet.

Cayce also gave a reading for Patricia Farrier, a 45-year-old woman who suffered from claustrophobia and a fear of being smothered. Patricia frequently suffered from acute shortness of breath, feeling that she was suffocating, and would sometimes lapse into a coma. Attuning himself psychically to the source of her anxieties, Cayce saw her as a young girl living in Fredericksburg, Virginia, in colonial times. Her name in that life was Geraldine Fairfax, and she was thirteen years old. Cayce told her that she had been playing in a cellar where seedlings, potatoes and herbs were stored for the winter months. Suddenly an earth tremor caused the floor of the farmhouse to collapse. The shelves in the farmhouse then fell in a heap, burying her beneath an avalanche of roots, bulbs and damp soil, and she was literally smothered to death. Cayce continued to correspond with Patricia Farrier, providing helpful advice about her health, until her death in January 1939.

Edgar Cayce gave some 2500 life readings between 1923 and 1945. Details of these readings are now housed in the library at the Association for Research and Enlightenment at Virginia Beach, Virginia. As a psychic and healer, Cayce was somehow able to utilize a state of trance in order to tap into previous incarnations, apparently at will. Cayce also came to believe that groups of souls could reincarnate collectively, and that people bound by ties of family, friendship or common interests would very likely be related, or connected to each other in some way, in successive incarnations.

The dream research of Dr. Guirdham

Like trance states, dreams can also provide us with apparent evidence of reincarnation. Few such incidences are more fascinating than those explored by Dr. Arthur Guirdham.

Dr. Guirdham was chief psychiatrist at Bath Hospital in England in 1961 when he first met a woman whom he has since referred to as "Mrs. Smith," in

order to conceal her identity. Dr. Guirdham described Mrs. Smith as a "perfectly sane, ordinary housewife," but since the age of twelve she had been suffering from frightening dreams of murder and massacre – dreams so intense that she would shriek loudly during her sleep.

Dr. Guirdham examined Mrs. Smith for symptoms of neurosis and found none, but after a few months of treatment she told Dr. Guirdham that she had written down her dreams when she was still a 13-year-old school girl. Because these notes contained details about people and names she had never heard of – things which continued to puzzle her – she allowed the psychiatrist to read them. What really amazed Dr. Guirdham was that these notes contained verses of songs written in medieval French, a subject that his patient had never studied at school. The notes also contained drawings of old French coins and jewelry, as well as specific references to individual people and the layout of particular buildings.

Mrs. Smith believed that her dreams referred to the 13th century and the region around Toulouse. This had been a stronghold of the Cathars, a group of Christians who believed in the religious power of catharsis, or purification, and who also believed in reincarnation and the Gnostic concept of the spiritual transcendence of the soul. Catharism was so strong in southern and western Europe that the Roman Catholic Church came to regard it as a serious threat to religious orthodoxy. It was branded a heretical movement, and a crusade was called against it.

Mrs. Smith was convinced that she had been a member of the Cathar community in Toulouse in a previous life. During her terrifying nightmares, she experienced being burned at the stake, and vividly recalled such details as the hissing of the flames and the intense bleeding from her body. She also described a crypt where prisoners had been held prior to their execution.

Dr. Guirdham contacted Professor Pere Nelli, a specialist medieval scholar at Toulouse University, who confirmed that details from Mrs. Smith's dream records seemed to provide an accurate account of the Cathars of Toulouse.

Later, in 1967, Dr. Guirdham decided to visit this region of southern France himself. Here, he was able to gain access to additional Cathar documents available only to specialist scholars and found that all of the details in Mrs. Smith's nightmares were accurate. Even the medieval songs which she had written down as a child were correct – word for word. And other details were impressively specific as well. For example, Mrs. Smith's dream notes indicated that Cathar priests did not always wear black garments, as had been previously thought, but sometimes wore garments that were blue or green. The specialist scholars were unaware of this particular fact when Mrs. Smith first recorded her dreams in 1944, and it was not officially documented until records from a local Inquisition were published by Professor Duvernoy of Toulouse University in 1966.

Later, Dr. Guirdham worked with another patient, whom he referred to as "Miss Clare Mills." Clare Mills had a recurrent reincarnational dream of fleeing from a castle and being led away to a burning pyre, and she too made very specific references to Cathar sacraments and ritual details. After extensive investigations Dr. Guirdham was able to trace her identity back to a woman named Esclarmonde, daughter of Raymond de Perella, whose chateau of Montsegur near the Pyrenees had been destroyed in 1244. In the same way that details in Mrs. Smith's dream notes were subsequently found to be factual, obscure names in Miss Mills's account were later verified in the records of the Inquisition.

If we accept the extraordinary evidence presented by Dr. Guirdham in his books *The Cathars and Reincarnation* and *We Are One Another*, it seems that groups of individuals who have shared a traumatic past – like the burning of heretics at the stake – can sometimes reincarnate collectively and then reconnect with each other at a future time and place. Why a cluster of medieval identities from southern France should be reborn in the city of Bath in England is difficult to explain, but Dr. Guirdham's documentation certainly suggests that we should remain open to the possibility of group reincarnation.

Hypnotic regression into past lives

One of the most fascinating aspects of reincarnation research
is the use of hypnosis to explore past lives.
Some of this research has been very inconclusive,
and seems to have uncovered fantasies from the subconscious
mind rather than authentic memories of personalities who
really did exist and historical events that really did take place.

ON THE OTHER HAND, there is evidence from the annals of hypnotic regression that demands an explanation. For some people investigating these cases, the concept of reincarnation provides the best answer.

The most famous pioneering case of this sort – the case that really drew international attention to the technique of hypnotic regression for the first time – was the story of Bridey Murphy.

Who was Bridey Murphy?

In November 1952, in the town of Pueblo, Colorado, a 29-year-old housewife named Virginia Tighe agreed to take part in an experiment involving a number of sessions of hypnosis. Morey Bernstein, a local hypnotist and businessman, said he would lead Mrs. Tighe backward in time using the hypnotic technique of age regression.

In the first hypnotic session she was encouraged to remember the toys she used to play with when she was just one year old; in the second session Bernstein told her that she would go back until she found herself in some other scene – "in some other place, in some other time." He also said that she would be able to describe her experiences and answer his questions.

This hypnotic technique seemed to reveal evidence of two past lives. The first of these was that of a child who had died while still a baby, but the second was far more detailed, and involved a person known as Bridget, or Bridey, Murphy. Mrs. Tighe herself was a native of Madison, Wisconsin, and had never visited Ireland or had anything much to do with any Irish people. However, her hypnotic regression seemed to suggest that in an earlier existence she had been a native of Cork, a city in southern Ireland. She had vivid recollections of everyday life in Ireland, and could name several relatives and regional locations as well as speak in a local Irish dialect.

According to the details revealed through hypnosis, Bridey Murphy had been born on December 20, 1798, the daughter of a barrister called Duncan Murphy and his wife, Kathleen. The Murphy family was Protestant. Bridey had a brother, Duncan Blaine, who was born in 1796. He later married Aimée, daughter of a lady called Mrs. Strayne, who ran a day school in Cork. Bridey attended this school when she was fifteen, "studying to be a lady." Under

hypnosis Mrs. Tighe provided the names of two of Bridey's friends, Mary Katherine and Kevin Moore, and described how she later married Sean Brian MacCarthy, son of a Catholic barrister, and went with him to live in Belfast. She even described the carriage trip to Belfast, passing through Mourne and Bailings Crossing – places too small to be found on any map, but which nevertheless did actually exist.

Further details were provided about which church Bridey attended in Belfast – St. Theresa's – which shops she visited for food and clothing, and even specific Irish dances and jigs that she enjoyed as entertainments. She also named three men she knew at Queens University. What was most fascinating was that Mrs. Tighe's Irish accent developed as the sessions progressed, and she frequently spoke in a quite specific dialect, using local words, phrases and pronunciations.

Bridey died in 1864 at the age of 66, after falling down some stairs and breaking her hip, but Mrs. Tighe nevertheless retained the memory of a man playing the uilleann pipes at her funeral. She then recalled details of her "intermission state" between lives, mentioning that deceased relatives didn't necessarily stay together and that she could travel from one location to another – places such as Cork and Belfast – simply by willing it be so. In due course she was told that the time had come for her to reincarnate, and she was reborn as the present-day Mrs. Tighe.

In 1956 Morey Bernstein published an account of his hypnotic regressions under the title *The Search for Bridey Murphy*. The book caused considerable controversy in the popular media, and became an instant bestseller. It was translated into numerous foreign languages and was later made into a film. Mrs. Tighe was referred to in the book under a pseudonym – Ruth Simmons – in order to protect her true identity.

It was not possible to verify the family details provided by Mrs. Tighe during her hypnotic regression – registers of births, deaths, and marriages were not introduced in Cork until 1864 – and it is surprising that Bridey could not recall her actual address in Belfast during the hypnotic sessions. However, it is impressive that she could provide specific Irish words and phrases, and also describe cultural practices that were unique to that period. Bridey also spoke of a rope company as well as a tobacco house in Belfast, which did actually exist, and she also correctly named the only two grocers trading in Belfast at the time.

Forty years later, the case of Bridey Murphy and Mrs. Tighe remains a fascinating mystery – a pioneering case in the literature of hypnotic regression into past lives. It is also worth mentioning that although Morey Bernstein was only an amateur hypnotist, he nevertheless regarded his explorations in hypnosis as a very serious pursuit, and spent a considerable amount of time with Professor Rhine and his staff at Duke University – a university widely acclaimed for the scientific study of extrasensory perception.

The case of Bridey Murphy remains among the most famous of all past-life regressions, but it is not an isolated instance.

Mrs. Williams and the Titanic

Doris Williams, a registered nurse who now works as a reflexologist, moved to California from her native Ohio in 1955. For most of her life she had suffered from an intense fear of deep water and ocean voyages. Once, during an ocean cruise to Hawaii, she suffered from such intense and overwhelming anxiety that she became very ill.

In 1960 Mrs. Williams visited a hypnotist at Venice Beach, California. She allowed herself to be hypnotized, and found herself aboard the ill-fated ocean liner *Titanic*, in April 1912. Her name at this time was Blackwell – she later expanded this to Stephen Weart Blackwell. Mrs. Williams didn't take her session very seriously, and thought that it might be just a fantasy from her subconscious mind. However, she was later intrigued to discover in her local library that a person named Stephen Weart Blackwell had indeed been a passenger on the *Titanic* – he was mentioned in Walter Lord's well-known book *A Night to Remember*. Mrs. Williams was very surprised by this, because she had never paid any attention to the idea of reincarnation before.

Several months later, Mrs. Williams became friendly with a hypnotherapist named Zelda Suplee, who was a charter member of the Association for Past-Life Research and Therapy in Riverside, California. Ms Suplee subsequently guided Mrs. Williams through another hypnotic regression in order to seek further information about Stephen Blackwell. During this hypnotic session Mrs. Williams assumed the identity of Stephen Blackwell and began to recount details of his life and work. Blackwell said that he was 43 years old, married, and employed by the Brown Shipping Company, located at 167 West State Street, Trenton, New Jersey. Here he worked in an office dealing with transport bills and shipping. Blackwell described his family background, and his initial desire

to go to medical school. He also mentioned that he had made several business trips to England as part of his work. Later in the session he began to describe events on the *Titanic* just prior to the sinking, after the disastrous collision with an iceberg: "There was a lot of noise ... I joined the people fully dressed in dark clothes ... I went on top facing the front of the ship, water to my left ... I watched lifeboats being lowered. There was a lot of crying, music – religious music ..."

Reliving these traumatic events did not help Doris Williams with her anxieties, but she gradually became more open to the possibility of a being the reincarnation of Stephen Blackwell. Meanwhile, Zelda Suplee began to track down as much documentation as she could find relating to the *Titanic* and its victims. After consulting with the president of the Oceanic Navigation and Research Society, Zelda Suplee was able to confirm that Stephen Weart Blackwell had indeed been one of the people who drowned in the sinking of the *Titanic,* and that he had worked for the Brown Shipley Company in Trenton: he had been the British representative of the American company. This information on Blackwell was not included in any published book Zelda Suplee could find on the *Titanic*. Also, as stated during the hypnotic regression, Stephen Blackwell had been 43 years old at the time of his death and had been returning to the United States after a business trip to Europe.

The work of Arnall Bloxham

Arnall Bloxham was a hypnotherapist who ran his practice from his home in Cardiff, Wales. He first began experimenting with hypnotic past-life regression in the 1940s. Bloxham was elected president of the British Society of Hypnotherapists in 1972, and was the subject of a BBC television documentary series on past lives. Bloxham regressed around 400 subjects into past lives; most of them were comparatively dull and uninteresting. However, one of his best subjects – Welsh housewife Jane Evans – experienced six past lives under hypnosis, some of them containing fascinating historical information.

Jane Evans had originally made contact with Bloxham because she was looking for a hypnotherapist to treat her rheumatism. She was not especially interested in reincarnation before her regressions, but some extraordinary material soon emerged. Under hypnosis, Jane Evans recalled these former lives:

- In the third century AD, she was Livonia, a tutor's wife, and lived in the Roman British city of Eboracum, otherwise known as York.
- She reincarnated as Rebecca, a young Jewish woman massacred in York in 1190.
- Later she was Alison, the teenage servant of a French merchant prince named Jacques Coeur. Alison died in 1451.
- Her next incarnation was Ann (1485–1536), a servant to Catherine of Aragon.
- In her next life, she was Ann Tasker (1665–1714), a serving girl living in London during the reign of Queen Anne.
- She then reincarnated as Sister Grace, nee Ellis, a nun in Maryland, USA, and died around 1920, prior to being reborn as Jane Evans.

Of all these, Jane Evans's incarnations as Livonia and Rebecca are perhaps the most intriguing. Under hypnosis, Jane Evans regressed to the year 286 AD, when she was Livonia, the wife of Titus – a tutor in poetry, Greek and Latin to Constantine, who would later become emperor of Rome. Livonia and Titus were converted to Christianity by a woodcarver named Albanus, and died violently during the reign of Diocletian. Details which emerged during this hypnotic regression were checked by Professor Brian Hartley of Leeds University, a specialist in Roman history, and found to be substantially correct. What is fascinating about this particular regression is that, if it is true, Constantine was in Britain in the year 286 AD. This is one of the "missing years" of Constantine's early life, about which historians have no documentation, and it is possible that Jane Evans has revealed a historical detail which may yet be verified by specialist research.

Jane Evans was regressed in front of television cameras as she re-entered her former life as Rebecca, a young Jewish mother in twelfth-century York. She recounted in a hypnotic state how she was massacred alongside many other Jews in a church crypt in 1190.

Rebecca's memories were extremely detailed and historically accurate. She mentioned how, as a Jew, she had been required to wear a badge identifying her as Jewish, and she also provided details of the Jewish money-lending trade in York and the nearby city of Lincoln. The most intense aspects of the hypnotic regression were associated with her memory of the massacre itself – she went on to describe how a large group of anti-Semitic Christian marauders killed every Jew they could find in York and also went on a fierce looting rampage. Through the identity of Rebecca, Mrs. Evans described how some Jewish parents had killed their own children to avoid them being slaughtered by the mob – a detail that proved to be historically accurate. Rebecca hid in a church crypt with her children, but they were all discovered and killed.

Following Jane Evans's detailed description of the massacre, the church where she died was identified by Professor Barrie Dobson as St Mary's in Castlegate. Professor Dobson was a specialist in Jewish history at York University, and the author of a book on the 1190 massacre. He commented that many of the details which emerged during the hypnotic session were available only to specialist scholars and were not known by the general public. However, an even more significant finding later emerged. At the time of the hypnotic regression it was thought that St Mary's Church did not have a crypt – crypts were rare in York. But during church renovations an ancient crypt was discovered on the site – dating to either the Norman or the Roman period, and

therefore predating the massacre in 1190. This discovery therefore confirmed an important detail of the past-life recall not available through any other source.

Cases such as those we have summarized here – and there are many more in the annals of past-life research – suggest that hypnosis can be used to uncover fascinating details of former incarnations. Past life memories are often very detailed and specific, and can sometimes be verified independently through specialized historical research – frequently involving sources of information not available to the person undergoing hypnosis.

However, several issues involving analyzing the reincarnational evidence in more detail need to be resolved. If a person has a strong reincarnational memory of a former life, does this necessarily mean that they were actually that person in a former incarnation, or are other factors involved? In the next chapter we will explore some of the different hypotheses and explanations relating to reincarnational memories.

Different views of reincarnation

There are several different ways of responding
to reincarnation evidence. It is important to emphasize that in
this brief introductory overview we are focusing on
reincarnation cases that have been put forward as genuine.

WE ARE ALL SEEKING an answer to a basic question, and that is: how can we account for cases such as those of the Pollock twins in England, Jane Evans's apparent previous life as Rebecca in York, and the birthmarks and specific memories which feature in the case of Victor Vincent? Obviously, claimed reincarnation cases that in reality are instances of intentional fraud or deception also exist, but they are of no use in helping us understand those cases which present a genuine mystery and which demand an explanation.

Who objects to the idea of reincarnation?

Some people will dismiss all instances of claimed reincarnation because they believe that such an idea is fundamentally incompatible with current scientific concepts relating to the brain and human perception. From their perspective, reincarnational memories must therefore be nothing other than delusional fantasies. Others will respond more from a religious or philosophical orientation, and say that the very idea of rebirth is alien to their personal belief system, and beyond what they can accept as true.

As we have already mentioned, most people holding an essentially materialistic view of life believe that reincarnation cannot possibly be true because there is no proof that the soul actually exists, and therefore there is nothing within a human being which can possibly reincarnate. According to this viewpoint, when we die our personal identity ceases to exist. It is also the end of conscious awareness, because human consciousness can only arise through the functioning of a living brain. In short, the idea that consciousness can survive physical death is impossible, so reincarnation is also impossible.

Another scientifically based objection to the idea of reincarnation is the fact that the world's population is increasing dramatically, and will probably double in the next 50 or 60 years. If this is the case, where will all the reincarnating souls actually come from? Surely, say these scientific skeptics, this means, even hypothetically, that there would be a shortage of reincarnating souls to accommodate all the people being born in the world …

Meanwhile, from a religious rather than a scientific perspective, some people also reject the concept of reincarnation purely on theological grounds. As we have already noted, most mainstream Christians and Muslims, and orthodox Jews, do not accept the idea of a reincarnating soul for doctrinal reasons.

According to these traditions, each individual soul is provided as a gift from God with the commencement of a new life, and after death the soul is destined either for Paradise or for some form of eternal torment or punishment. Put simply, there is no possibility of getting a "second chance" after you die …

Answering the skeptics

Contrary to the viewpoints we have just described, some reincarnation supporters claim that belief in rebirth is not only compatible with science, but is actually supported by it. After all, scientists as well as those who believe in reincarnation recognize that, subject to the currently accepted laws of physics, matter and/or energy can never be destroyed – it simply changes form. Just as physical matter can be transmuted into energy and vice versa, it is equally possible that the identity or individual consciousness of a person may become more fluid or energy-like after death, and then flow into another physical form.

The well-known doctor and philosopher Dr. Elisabeth Kübler-Ross – who believes in reincarnation – says she regards physical death rather like discarding an old set of clothes. Once death claims the physical body, she says, human consciousness is released and is then free to continue on its way. This view is based on the idea that consciousness or spirit – which we are equating here with energy – is really the ultimate reality in the universe, and matter is just its external veneer, reflected in the full spectrum of physical forms that we perceive in the everyday world.

Dr. Kübler-Ross's view of the liberated human spirit is supported by current research into near-death experiences. Here, many subjects who have been declared clinically dead by their doctors and who have subsequently revived and "returned to life" report that their conscious awareness continues after their apparent physical "death." In describing their experience of the transition through death, they tend to describe their essential identity – *the person they feel they really are as human beings* – more in spiritual than in physical terms. They also frequently report that their conscious awareness and mental functioning are actually enhanced rather than restricted while they are in an out-of-body state, which is exactly the reverse of what one would expect if consciousness were to die with the brain at death!

With regard to the number of reincarnating souls in an ever-expanding population, this does at first seem to be a major objection to the possibility of reincarnation. However, there are different ways of responding to this issue. Firstly, in terms of population, we are not yet at a point where the number of people currently living on the planet exceeds the total number of people who have ever lived in the past. From a pro-reincarnation point of view, this may mean that more individual souls are reincarnating now than has been possible in the past, because the expanding population base means more bodies are becoming available! Also, many Hindus believe that some people are now experiencing their first lifetime as human beings, having reincarnated from previous animal and other non-human forms. This further complicates the mathematical question of how many souls are available for reincarnation at any particular time, and where these souls come from, but it is certainly an issue we cannot ignore. If all forms of life are interconnected at a sub-nuclear level, as physicists now believe, perhaps we should remain open to the possibility that the full spectrum of living forms –plants, animals and human beings – may be part of an ongoing universal flow of life energy which is fundamentally without boundaries and without constriction, a life flow which has no clear beginning and no foreseeable end.

Who or what reincarnates?

Even among those who accept reincarnation as true, there are different perspectives on what actually occurs. The first viewpoint, one which is widely held both in the East and by contemporary New Agers, is that each human being is undertaking an individual spiritual journey which will take many lifetimes – culminating in a state of spiritual self-realization or transcendence. We can think of this as each individual soul gradually wending its way toward God, and going through numerous reincarnations in order to learn the "lessons of life" as part of this seemingly endless journey. In the East it is widely accepted that sometime in the future – either in this life or in a future life – each of us will reap what we have sown, the consequences of both our thoughts and our actions. Our future reincarnations will reflect the positive or negative karma accumulated during our present life on Earth, just as our present life situation reflects the accumulated karmic debt of our past incarnations. This concept, then, is one of an individual human soul experiencing a succession of individual reincarnations on the spiritual journey back to God.

However, for those who draw more on the esoteric interpretations of Buddhist and Hindu scriptures, there is another important consideration – that ultimately there is only one Consciousness, or spiritual reality, in the entire universe. According to these teachings, this unifying and all-encompassing God-consciousness is ultimately all that exists. Whether we refer to this spiritual reality as God, Allah, Brahman or Unity Consciousness is of little concern – the important point is that all sentient beings have their origin within this Sacred Oneness. This means that although we regard ourselves as individual human beings and think of ourselves as having independent lives and separate spiritual destinies, at a universal level we are really all interconnected – we are literally all One. Our sense of individual identity is actually an illusion.

A drop in the Ocean of Being

There is a well-known spiritual metaphor which compares each individual human life to a drop within an infinite ocean, the ocean in turn symbolizing God, or Sacred Oneness. The key point here is that the spiritual essence or "identity" of both the drop and the ocean are fundamentally the same. This in turn implies that it is not the individual soul that reincarnates. Rather, we can regard each human incarnation as simply a manifestation of the one Universal Consciousness. According to this interpretation, at the universal level of being we are not only ourselves — we are also each other. Potentially, everything that has ever existed in the world, every life that has ever been lived throughout human history, is nothing other than memories within the Universal Mind of God. Reincarnational memories can therefore be interpreted as memories which derive from this level of Universal Consciousness. People entering a hypnotic state of trance may begin to experience former incarnations because they are tapping into this universal memory bank — and in some cases there is clear historical evidence that these particular identities have actually lived in former times — but ultimately all memories are One Memory, and all lives are One Life. This is the Unity Consciousness explanation of reincarnation.

What if reincarnation is true?

Let's assume for a moment that reincarnation is not just a
theory, but actually happens. This means that whether we
believe in reincarnation or not becomes irrelevant.

REINCARNATION IS THEN REGARDED simply as a universal principle relating to
life, birth and death – a principle much the same as the law of gravity or the law
of the conservation of energy. This being the case, would we live our lives
differently?

What if we are all spiritually connected?

One thing is certain. If reincarnation is true and we are all interconnected at a
universal spiritual level, any harm or misfortune we bring into the world is
ultimately directed also at ourselves. The Dalai Lama offers some fascinating
insights on how we should live our lives in relation to reincarnation, especially in
terms of the need for tolerance and compassion in our dealings with other
people. In his view, we should extend the instinctive bond we feel with members
of our own immediate family to the broad sweep of humanity, because through
our numerous lifetimes on this Earth – experienced through the endless cycles of
rebirth – we are actually all related to each other. Our father or mother in this

lifetime may have been our son or daughter in an earlier life. Our friend, neighbor or antagonist this time around may have been someone we knew in an earlier period. Similarly, the sense of trust, closeness, enmity or resentment we experience now may be the karmic consequence of something which happened a long time ago.

According to the Dalai Lama, we are all one family – one collective consciousness – whether we choose to recognize it or not. This means that we have to learn to work through our countless interactions with each other –in love or war, in friendship or compassion, or hostility, resentment, jealousy or envy – until we finally realize that all our challenges and battles are really with ourselves. This is certainly a powerful message for the troubled times in which we now live.

A final thought

As we have acknowledged earlier, many people in the West reject the very idea that their present lives may have been influenced by previous incarnations. Some also cannot accept the Eastern idea that we live in the country of our birth, have the parents we have, and find ourselves in a situation of wealth or poverty, health or ill-health as a result of our thoughts and actions during former lives on Earth.

However, even if we reject the concept of reincarnation, we can all seek to improve the nature of our interactions with other people. We can all begin to act as if we are part of one human family and one collective consciousness. In this way, whether we accept the idea of reincarnation or not, the world will certainly become a better place.

Glossary

AKASA In Hinduism, the fifth element, Spirit, which encompasses the other four – Earth, Water, Fire and Air.

ATMAN The spiritual self which resides within Brahman – the human soul.

BODHISATTVAS In Mahayana Buddhism, spiritually enlightened beings who have chosen to reincarnate.

BRAHMAN In Hinduism, the Godhead, or ultimate spiritual reality.

CHURINGA Among the Australian Aborigines, a sacred representation (usually made of wood or stone) of a totemic object, used during ceremonial initiations.

DALAI LAMA The spiritual leader of the Tibetan people. The present Dalai Lama, Tenzin Gyatso, is the fourteenth such leader and was awarded the Nobel Prize for Peace in 1989.

DHARMA Sanskrit word for one's ethical obligation or duty. Following the path of dharma means following a path of spiritual action.

HERESY Any religious doctrine or teaching which departs from orthodoxy.

HYPNOTIC REGRESSION Technique of hypnosis used to regress subjects to an earlier time in their present lives, and then beyond, into past incarnations.

KA Ancient Egyptian term for the soul.

KARMA Sanskrit term for the spiritual principle of cause and effect. Positive thoughts and actions create good karma, and negative thoughts and actions create bad karma.

METEMPSYCHOSIS Reincarnation into a human or animal form (it means to reincarnate into an animal form, not the belief in that).

MOKSHA Knowledge of one's true inner self. This is a state of spiritual enlightenment.

NEAR-DEATH EXPERIENCES Visionary experiences reported by subjects who have been declared clinically dead but who have subsequently revived.

NIRVANA Enlightenment or spiritual self-realization.

REINCARNATION The belief that one's identity or "consciousness" survives physical death, and may be reborn in different physical bodies in a succession of future lives. In the Buddhist and Hindu traditions, the nature of these future lives is determined according to the law of karma.

SAMSARA Hindu term for the karmic cycle of life, death and rebirth.

TRANSMIGRATION Another word for metempsychosis (see above).

TULKU In Mahayana Buddhism, someone who is considered to be the reincarnation of a specific other person, god or spirit.

UNITY CONSCIOUSNESS The experience of Oneness with God. According to the mystical traditions, this is all that really exists.

WHEEL OF REBIRTH A Hindu and Buddhist concept incorporating belief in reincarnation and in the law of karma, in which one undergoes a succession of births, deaths, and rebirths until the spiritual lessons of life have been learned and spiritual liberation has been achieved. The person who achieves spiritual liberation from the wheel of rebirth has no further need to reincarnate.

Further reading

Bernstein, Morey, *The Search for Bridey Murphy*, Doubleday, New York 1965

Christie-Murray, David, *Reincarnation: Ancient Beliefs and Modern Evidence*, Prism Press, Dorset 1985

Cranston, Sylvia, *Reincarnation: The Phoenix Fire Mystery*, Theosophical University Press, Pasadena, California 1994

Dalai Lama (with Jean-Claude Carrière), *Violence & Compassion*, Doubleday, New York 2001

Dalai Lama, *My Land and My People*, Warner Books, New York 1997

Guirdham, Arthur, *The Cathars and Reincarnation*, Spearman, London 1970

Guirdham, Arthur, *We Are One Another*, Spearman, London 1974

Langley, Noel, *Edgar Cayce on Reincarnation*, Warner Books, New York 1988

Motoyama, Hiroshi, *Karma and Reincarnation*, Piatkus, London 1998

Rogo, D. Scott, *The Search for Yesterday*, Prentice-Hall, Englewood Cliffs, New Jersey 1985

Shroder, Tom, *Old Souls: The Scientific Evidence for Past Lives*, Simon & Schuster, New York 1999

Stevenson, Ian, *Twenty Cases Suggestive of Reincarnation*, University of Virginia Press, Charlottesville, Virginia 1995

TenDam, Hans, *Exploring Reincarnation*, Arkana, London 1990

Wambach, Helen, *Reliving Past Lives*, Harper & Row, New York 1978

This edition published by Barnes & Noble Inc.,
by arrangement with Lansdowne Publishing Pty Ltd

2002 Barnes & Noble Books

ISBN 0-7607-3234-5

M 10 9 8 7 6 5 4 3 2 1

Commissioned by Deborah Nixon
Text: Nevill Drury
Illustrator: Penny Lovelock, with additional illustrations by Sue Ninham and
Joanna Davies
Cover illustration: Penny Lovelock
Designer: Avril Makula
Editor: Sarah Shrubb
Production Manager: Jane Kirby
Project Coordinator: Kate Merrifield

Set in Granjon and Arbitrary on QuarkXPress
Printed in Singapore by Tien Wah Press (Pte) Ltd